JUST IN CASE...

SCHOOL SUCKS

TOOLS FOR TRANSFORMATION

DR. MICHELLE DONAH, PH.D.

Copyright © 2017 Dr. Michelle Donah, Ph.D.
Interior Art Credit: Ellen Welk

All rights reserved. No part of this book may be used or reproduced by any means, graphic, electronic, or mechanical, including photocopying, recording, taping or by any information storage retrieval system without the written permission of the author except in the case of brief quotations embodied in critical articles and reviews.

Balboa Press books may be ordered through booksellers or by contacting:

Balboa Press
A Division of Hay House
1663 Liberty Drive
Bloomington, IN 47403
www.balboapress.com
1 (877) 407-4847

Because of the dynamic nature of the Internet, any web addresses or links contained in this book may have changed since publication and may no longer be valid. The views expressed in this work are solely those of the author and do not necessarily reflect the views of the publisher, and the publisher hereby disclaims any responsibility for them.

Any people depicted in stock imagery provided by Thinkstock are models, and such images are being used for illustrative purposes only.
Certain stock imagery © Thinkstock.

ISBN: 978-1-5043-8729-3 (sc)
ISBN: 978-1-5043-8731-6 (e)

Print information available on the last page.

Library of Congress Control Number: 2017913876

Balboa Press rev. date: 09/07/2017

Contents

The Truth v
Testimonials vii
Dedication ix
Acknowledgements x
Foreword xi
Introduction xv

Part 1: WHY School Sucks 1
Chapter 1:   A Day in the Life 3
Chapter 2:   Your Brain's Inside Boss 5
Chapter 3:   Working Memory 9
Chapter 4:   To Med or Not to Med? 11

Part 2: WHAT You Can Do About It - Secret Brain Hacks 13
Chapter 5:   Expand Your Capacity 15
Chapter 6:   Let's Talk About Stress, Baby! 18
Chapter 7:   Be About It! 25
Chapter 8:   Let Your Fingers Do the Talking 29
Chapter 9:   Fuel Your Brain! 32
Chapter 10: Move Your Body! 35
Chapter 11: Be Your Own Best Advocate! 38
Chapter 12: Be Your Own Expert! 42
Chapter 13: Rev-Up Your Reading! 43
Chapter 14: Super-Size Your Results 45
Chapter 15: Get a Coach! 48

Bonus: Test-Taking Guide 51
Chapter 16: Wrapping It All Up 53
Chapter 17: Some Helpful Websites to Visit: 54

The Truth

If you read only one page out of this book, do make it this one!

The Truth is, my friend, that what you perceive about yourself is not the truth. You have been misperceiving through a lens of accumulated past failures. School doesn't really suck, but it sure seems that way. Why? Because of your past experiences.

You are not your past experiences. If, however, you base your evaluation of your own abilities and school experiences on things that didn't go well, then a lens forms. If you bought this book, and I titled this book just to attract you, then there is the perception that school sucks for you, and most likely that you lack certain abilities to succeed in school.

Let me dismantle that untruth for you right now. Your perception is based on the past. The past does not exist right now; it is only a memory, or a filtered experience hanging out in your mind. It's not your current reality.

Your reality is right now, my friend. And you have choices. So many options are available to you, but you have to release your current illusion that there is something wrong with you and school. There is nothing wrong. There are no mistakes. Your truth is not, "I can't" or "I suck," or even "School sucks." That title was just a ruse to draw you into the truth.

Your truth is that you are infinite potential, powerful and magnificent.

The explanations and solutions in this book are designed to help you tap into that truth and your infinite potential nature. It's already within you.

My hope is that this book called to you for some reason, and you are ready to work toward your infinite Potential.

Please reach out to me. I am here to help.

I Love You!
Michelle E. Donah, Ph.D.
iheart2learn.com

Testimonials

Dr. Donah is by far the most nurturing and one of the most intellectual academics I have ever come into contact with. As a student, I felt her constant support, which helped tremendously, and also helped me gain confidence in the classroom and in myself. The unconventional, yet highly productive ways to learn, test taking strategies, and ways to deal with stress/anxiety make Dr. Donah such a upstanding teacher, mentor, and coach.
J.J., student, former mentee

Dr. Donah has a special gift helping children and teenagers understand the nature of their challenges in ways that help them engage with empowering interventions. She has encouraged her clients to see themselves in a positive light. She guides them with new thoughts and behaviors necessary to change their lives significantly. She has been the change factor for many youth, redirecting their futures from potential tragedy to success.
Dr. Carol Armstrong, Psy.D.

Having Dr. Donah as my son's life coach was a game changer.She taught him strategies to help him become and stay organized without the use of typical ADHD medications. By putting Dr. Donah's concepts to use, he became more proactive at approaching his teachers for help in class and is now a more confident and independent student.
T.C., parent

My son has been suffering through school for years until we met Michelle Donah. He couldn't seem to translate his natural intelligence into good grades which made him an anxious and unmotivated student. From the moment I met Michelle, her energy had me convinced that she would have my son's back. Michelle met him once a week, to go over his weekly plan. She taught him how to study and kept me in the loop of the process.
My son has been transformed into a happy, successful student and is even looking forward to returning for his senior year.
I have read the book and it's absolutely perfect! It describes exactly what the student goes trough, that he/she is not alone and assures that there are solutions to each and every struggle the student may face.

The book is geared towards students but is equally successful in communicating to parents and teachers what is going on in the mind of their children and students.

Absolutely a must read!
S.S., parent

Michelle Donah was an important influence that kept me afloat throughout my first year of high school during an especially crucial time of school; the transition year from middle school to high school. The biggest difference I noticed when switching from middle school was how much freedom you get during the day with study periods, and with that freedom comes with a lot of responsibilities. She helped me stay focused on completing assignments during free periods, instead of hanging out with my friends. She showed me the importance of doing some work at school and that helped keep me calm and not get overwhelmed at night with too much homework. She also showed me how to organize my computer to set reminders, daily tasks, and be much more organized, which helped me stay on track with all my assignments. Teachers don't usually teach you how to do that so I was struggling with so many things to remember. It's not all work though, she also believes that there should be time to just chill out and let yourself relax. Furthermore, she doesn't only help people through school assignments or time management, Dr. Donah is a very spiritual being and can help you feel less stressed. My school year was much more enjoyable and successful. Infinite love and gratitude.
E.E., student

Simply put: Dr. Donah understands kids. She understands their inner and outer lives; she understands how to inspire and encourage and connect with them. More than anything, what I admire about Dr. Donah is how she advocates for her clients. She treats young people as the best version of themselves, always offering support and accountability. While some academic coaches are obsessed with grades and standardized test scores, Dr. Donah builds in her clients the habits of mind that translate to success inside the classroom and beyond. Versed in cognitive science and holistic wellness techniques, Dr. Donah possesses the skill set to work well with a range of students. I can say, without reservation, that she has changed the lives of many students.
Dr. Kellen Graham, Dean of Academics, Cannon School

Dedication

With tremendous love, I dedicate this book to the two Carols in my life, Dr. Carol Donah, Ph.D. and Dr. Carol Armstrong, Psy.D. Your loving ways have made and are making a huge difference in this world. So Much Love.

Acknowledgements

Dear Boys, Thank you for teaching me everything I know. I love you all so much. I was set up to be your advisor, and it was you who advised me. For this, I am forever grateful. Clayton, Asil, Rob, Daniel, Zachary, Thomas, Michael, George, Donovan, Jamie and William, I wish you all the biggest and brightest futures as you do your work in making this world a bright and beautiful place. It is an honor to share paths with you.

Thank you all who contributed financially to the publication of this book, and for helping me see it through.

Sharon Faw, for your belief in me, Thank you.

Dr. Darren Weissman, Infinite Love and Gratitude for your unwavering support and belief in this project.

Ellen Welk, Thank you for bringing your artistic talents to the table, and for helping me through the process.

Thank you, Greta Berg, for your brilliant contributions toward helping me get this started and the again in finalizing it.

Though my name may be in print, this book is really a collaborative effort, and I can now say, it takes a village to raise a book!

Infinite Love and Gratitude,
Dr. Donah

Foreword by Dr. Darren Weissman

Lasting change and building genuine happiness begin with understanding that we live in an interactive reality whose architect is the mind. Otherwise put, the way you think about yourself directly influences how you experience your life. To change our relationship with school we must first begin with our thoughts. This will occur when you align your choices with your heart's desire. Welcome to your inner genius!

School isn't your problem. School is your portal. The challenges and struggles you've been experiencing with school are a doorway to the next greatest version of yourself. As the late Dr. Wayne Dyer stated, "When you change the way you view things, the things that you view will begin to change." By picking up this book and applying its principles, you have made a courageous choice to boldly step into a bright and abundant future.

My dear friend and colleague, Dr. Michelle Donah is offering you a powerful new perspective combined with simple tools to enhance your confidence and capabilities. She ultimately is sharing a way to choose love in the face of fear and thus provide a prism through which you can learn to see, feel, and hear every challenge or stressful situation – school and beyond – as an opportunity to evolve and transform your life. Creating sustainable change can be likened to the difference between reading about driving a car and getting behind the wheel. Experience is the greatest teacher. To begin our adventure, let's probe beneath the surface to reveal the root causes of why we struggle with school in the first place.

The heart of the matter of falling behind with homework, struggling with test taking, having difficulty with comprehending what you read, being unable to focus, and getting bad grades has another purpose and meaning beyond the experience itself. This topic can be a very slippery slope; however, asking what I call the Truth Question helps to shape-shift the judgment you may be holding towards yourself and school into a moment of conscious discernment and awakening. It is this single Truth Question that changes the entire game of school and thus compels you to take action and discover the wisdom and power of your emotions: "Given the opportunity, would you ever choose to create your life, a day, or even a single moment where school sucked? Would you choose to feel stupid? Would you choose to get poor grades? Would you choose to struggle with concentrating, feel overwhelmed, or be stricken with anxiety or panic when it came to any aspect of school?" The answer is obvious, and always: "Hell No!"

Knowing that we never choose to be stuck, struggle, or suffer, yet everyone on one level or another has these types of experiences, leads us to ask: "What's causing school to suck?" and even further, "What can I do about it?".

Let's begin with our beautiful brain. As amazing as it is, the brain is not designed to know the difference between a memory, reality, or imagination. When stressed by a poor diet, dehydration, inadequate sleep, lack of movement, and overwhelming circumstances going on at home or in life, our brain goes into survival mode. In a split second – clear, calm, and confident thoughts get hacked – and our brain is immediately sent into a state of protection and shut down. It is in this fear based reactive mindscape that our ability to learn and process information is turned off. This reactive process of shut down within your brain is not a choice . . . rather, it's the design and evolutionary nature of the mind and body. It's time to stop beating yourself up and start to build yourself up. It's not your fault that school sucks. However, even though it's not your fault, you are the hub to every spoke in your life. Before we get to where we desire to be – rocking it out in school – we must acknowledge and honor where we are as our starting point. Make the bold choice to take responsibility for your life experiences. This book will provide you with effective tools for owning your power.

What may appear to be a negative experience of poor memory, attention deficit, or dyslexia is what I refer to as The G.A.P. (The Gratitude Action Potential). The G.A.P. is a moment of subconscious protection that simultaneously graces us with the opportunity to learn, grow, and change in a way that would otherwise never be known. So many of the negative thought patterns we buy into about ourselves and others are emotionally charged memories and core limiting beliefs. These memories and beliefs, when activated, rise to the surface of our conscious reality and take on a life of their own.

If you believe a limiting belief your life becomes a lie. You are not your thoughts. You are not your feelings. You are not your beliefs. You are the creator of these and so much more. There is greatness in you! Just as the strongest trees live in the strongest winds, the stress you're experiencing in school is empowering your roots to dig deeper and you to reach higher. It's time to change the core limiting beliefs of your life into a core of infinite potential.

The book you are holding is an action step that will equip you with practical tools, strategies, and understanding of how to transform your relationship with school. Get ready to transcend and breakthrough walls of fear, self-judgment, and hatred. Walk the path and you'll discover awaiting you just around the bend is a bright and abundant future.

Stay curious my friends. It is your nature thrive. Lean into school with all you've got. Never ever give up. Your best is always enough. You want to succeed because you can. Dr. Michelle Donah's knowledge and passionate way of teaching and writing distill conscious learning into a practical philosophy for living a life you love to live. You've got this!

Keep shining bright!

With Infinite Love & Gratitude~

Dr. Darren Weissman
Best Selling Author of The Power of Infinite Love & Gratitude,
Developer of The LifeLine Technique®

Introduction

Dear Student,

I am so grateful you are picking up this book! Thank you!

I want you to know how perfect and wonderful you are. Yes, you!

Maybe you have difficulty with school, or maybe you have ADHD or another learning challenge. You might just be under the impression that school simply "sucks." But you know what? **There is nothing wrong with you.** I want you to take a minute and set aside anything negative you have been told, especially stuff like, "You're not working up to your potential." Sometimes your parents or teachers think "your potential" is the way they themselves actually think and do things. There isn't anything wrong with that either. They're doing their best with what they know.

Here's a thought: what if the world now needs new thinkers, people who think differently, people who keep their eyes open to the realm of unlimited possibilities and use their imaginations?

It turns out that the game has changed and there are new rules. We absolutely need people who can solve problems using an intelligence other than traditional school formulas, people who do not limit themselves to just one way of doing things. In short: **The World NEEDS YOU**--more than you can imagine!

The truth is, my friend, that you are fabulous and you have a purpose for being here. You are here to change the world in a way that only you and your way of thinking can.

In the meantime, you might wonder why the heck I wrote this book just for you, when I know reading might just not be your "thing." No worries. **I'm keeping it all brief--just the way you like it.** You can read it all, or just the parts that mean something to you. This is **your** book, and how you read it is up to you.

The goal of this book is to provide you with information on ways you can both understand and navigate your personal uniqueness as a learner. You can allow your natural abilities and ways of solving problems to shine through while you do your best to negotiate the standards set up for you. Part 1 is an explanation of some of the biggest reasons school sucks for many. Part 2 is all about the solutions, and you get to pick and choose your own! I believe in you, I have confidence in you, and, by the end of this book, you will have the same for yourself.

Infinite Love and Gratitude!

P.S. Just in case you really dislike reading, I've designed some **shortcuts for this book**. This is YOUR book. Flip through and take what you like.

Just in Case:

Homework sucks!
read: Chapters 2,3 & 8

Tests suck!

read: Chapters 7,8,9
plus Test-taking bonus guide

Reading sucks!
read: Chapters 3,7,13

My teacher hates me!
read: Chapters 1,2,3,6,11,12

Focusing sucks!
read: Chapters 1,2,3, 5,6, 13

Grades suck!
read: Chapter 14
plus Test-taking bonus guide

Part 1:

Chapter 1:

A Day in the Life

Picture this (you've been there before):

You're in class. All of a sudden you discover that you have left something very important (report or supplies) at home. Right on your desk too!

FACEPALM!

To make matters worse, you're late to school because your alarm clock once again let you down and it took you a long time to wake up, let alone get ready. Ugh.

You get back a test or paper, and it's way worse than you thought. The paper is riddled with teacher ink, probably red, and you missed stuff you never even saw before. Needless to say, your teacher gives you that look, you know the one I'm talking about. (Not to mention what your parents will say when they see the grade….) UGH!

Determined to never let it happen again, you decide to do better the next time. But then you get stuck…

So you take a break…

Okay, just a little more break…

Oh wow! It's 10 p.m. already? How did that just happen?

Just do your best, and start it all over the next day.

This goes on. Same plot, different day. It's like a hamster wheel where the same terrible events just keep playing over and over again. Except it's just getting worse. Eventually everyone's mad at you.

Eventually school and life can become a real drag. It can really suck. Your parents might take away your phone and video games. You can't hang out or chat with your friends. You feel bad about yourself, especially when you look around and everyone seems to be doing better than you. Adults and even other peers in your life make assumptions about your intelligence. You make assumptions about your intelligence, saying to yourself, "I'm just not that smart, I guess…." You get dragged down and the very thought of doing school work prompts your heart rate to increase and your palms to sweat. Sound familiar?

If you could do better, you would, right?

If you answered, "Yes," or "*Duh*!," then I have some solutions for you. Let's start with the fact that maybe your brain just needs a stronger director, an "Inside Boss" that coordinates and plans the pieces and gets them all working together.

Chapter 2:

Your Brain's Inside Boss

Has anyone ever called you *lazy*, *unmotivated*, or *behaviorally challenged*?

Huh. Well, let's step back and think about it. **Was it laziness and poor behavior, or, rather, was it a lack of planning and thinking ahead that caused you to falter, slow down, or make a hasty decision?** Do you get excited about something and have difficulty waiting your turn to share about it? Do your social skills lack finesse according to others?

If you answered yes to any of these questions, you're going to want to know about *executive functions*.

Did you know that something called your **executive functions** account for more of your academic performance than intelligence does? **Your grades are probably based mostly on your following instructions and turning an assignment in on time rather than on your actual ability and performance.** Most grades measure what we call obedience or adherence to standard rules, not necessarily your naturally brilliant and unlimited intelligence.

Chances are, especially if you are reading this, you're rather intelligent but perhaps earning some low scores in school. "But how can that be," you ask?

You think, "If I were smarter I'd do better," right?

Not necessarily. Due to any number of factors, **you might just have poor executive function (inside boss) skills.**

There is a large variety of names for this inside boss. Some experts refer to it as *executive function,* or *executive functioning,* or *executive functions, blah, blah blah*. There are as many terms for this as there are holes in Sponge Bob. What really matters to you is what they do. They direct your actions, **like a boss.**

They help you:

*organize your materials
*keep your room and workspace tidy
*plan your time
*start tasks
*end one task and start another
*sustain your focus on one task through completion
*solve problems (both math problems and people problems)
*read a whole paragraph and comprehend and remember it
*think ahead to plan your actions and their potential consequences (good or ugly)
*control impulsivity

In the best case scenario, your brain operates as a well-orchestrated masterpiece!

Basically, it's a whole lot of stuff.

When it all works together, under a good leader, a good director, guess what? You feel A-mazing! You can get stuff done, and even find it and know when and how to do it. Good brain conductivity makes you unstoppable!

Some people want to point out a specific space in the brain where these functions supposedly take place. They allocate much of this activity to a space in the front of the brain called the **prefrontal cortex.** And it's true, a lot of this activity does involve that frontal lobe. Other parts of the brain do engage and interact, but for the most part, the executive functions entail the involvement of the prefrontal cortex.

There's a guy named Phineas Gage who led a positive and productive life as a railroad foreman back in the 1800s. While working, he took a three-foot iron rod through the front portion of his head.

Ouch! Right?

While he lived to tell about the incident and was able to resume his daily activities, there was a huge change in his performance. He could no longer remember his appointments or keep track of his time. It became difficult for him to hold down a job like he had before. Though he was physically able and intelligent, his brain was unable to sequence and organize his tasks. **It's like his "inside boss" was out to lunch—permanently.** It's actually our friend Phineas who led brain scientists to locate the organization and management piece, the inside boss, of the front part of the brain.

If Phineas's struggle sounds real to you, it's because the section of the brain changed by Phineas's injury has to do with his executive functions--the very same skills that basically determine a huge amount of school success.

You are smart and perfectly capable of performing all of your tasks.

When it comes time to settle down and perform tasks like homework or a project, your brain becomes overwhelmed by the process. **It's not actually the difficulty level of the problem, it's the number of steps and how and when to use them that bogs you down.** You might get started and then frustrated, or you might get going on a math problem and then exhaust your capacity to sequence your steps and think clearly at the same time. You might start reading and completely lose what you read, or get distracted by one of your own thoughts.

Executive functions also play a role in your social life and how you interact with others. You may even get into social situations and get overwhelmed by too much going on around you, and your inside boss forgets social cues about how to respond appropriately. Interrupting others, blurting stuff out, feeling awkward in a group, not being sure how to respond--they are all matters of processing social cues, and sometimes it's simply too much to take in all at once. Add social media to the picture and we have an overload of sensory and content intake to process. Sometimes it just feels like too much, and shutting down seems like, feels like, the best possible option.

All of this **pressure, a.k.a. overwhelm**, can even make you **anxious** in certain situations. Anxiety can feel like anything from you'd rather not be there to your heart beating really fast and your palms sweating. Sometimes even just thinking about those situations can make you feel that way in advance.

Knowing and understanding that you might just be on information overload can help. Believing that there's something wrong with you and avoiding social interaction for this reason can increase your fears. Some of the tools in Part 2 of this book will help lessen those fears and empower you to engage more fully.

With explanation and some practice building up your inside boss, these functions can be improved and so can the quality of your life! So stay seated, and enjoy the ride. But first, let's look at **working memory and how it makes or breaks your inside boss**. Hang tight!

Chapter 3:

Working Memory

Working memory isn't exactly "memory" as you know it. It's not about your ability to memorize stuff. **Working memory is the ability to hold onto information for the split second it takes to sequence and manipulate steps, forward and backward, and thus to solve problems, think and plan ahead, arrange your space, and arrange your time.** These skills totally make or break your inside boss. These totally impact your ability to stick with a task, to start it and finish it and to "pay attention" to what you are doing.

Imagine a boss who can't see the big picture, or make plans, or remember what he just did let alone where he put...wait, what was it he was just holding? That makes for a scattered boss, right? The inside boss relies on that split second memory or *active attention* capacity called *working memory*. Picture links of a chain that all must fit together in order to work. If just one of those links doesn't grasp onto the next link, the whole process crumbles. Kind of like a bad night of homework, right? If you miss just one piece, the whole thing falls apart. It's like a frustration fest just waiting to happen.

Remember, working memory is your ability to instantaneously retain particles of information in order to link them for problem solving. It's like the places on a chain where the links interlock with each other, and the ability to use that chain for meaningful purpose. The links of the chain may all be there, but if they don't sync up efficiently enough, they weaken things like your organization and problem-solving. **Things like math and reading can seem really hard.** When these steps turn into multi-step processes, like around 5th or 6th grade, tasks can appear even more difficult, only because there is more room for slippage and error. More of your performance outcome hinges on the ability to link and hold larger units The greater your working memory capacity, the more you can handle these problem-solving tasks **like a boss.**

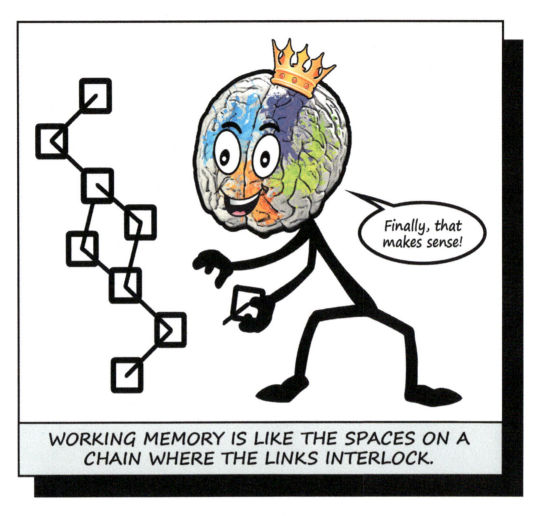

WORKING MEMORY IS LIKE THE SPACES ON A CHAIN WHERE THE LINKS INTERLOCK.

Many things can disrupt working memory. Biological brain development, nutrition, genetics, your body's chemistry, physical health, and emotional stress all impact this capacity for your brain to perform at its very best. Some other things may be interfering with your ability to perform your best, such as dysgraphia (writing difficulties), dyslexia (reading difficulties), or processing speed. The case remains that **the ability to understand the big and small pictures, to self-regulate, and to plan for your optimal expression of knowledge (all working memory tasks) still rules your performance.**

Here's the really good news: working memory, your executive function capacity, can be strengthened, which helps your inside boss direct the movement. Part 2, Chapter 1 will let you know how.

Chapter 4:

To Med or Not to Med?
That is a Good Question.

Let me be clear: I am not an expert on medication. I am, however, an expert on empowering you to know your choices and to make well-informed decisions with the help of your parents. Some of you may already take prescribed medication. Keep in mind that there are different classes of medication: some are stimulants and some are non-stimulants. If you are prescribed medication, it is important to know which one.

Many doctors like to prescribe the stimulant kind because they and your parents like to see quick results like better focus, better attention, and getting things done in less time. Most people feel more alert on this type of medication and it can make it easier to sit still and get things done. Parents seem pleased and teachers like the sitting still part, so they think the problem is solved.

Not all people who take medication enjoy it; they feel a part of their personality or creativity slips away. Most of my clients admit they would really prefer to go back to being themselves as opposed to making everyone else happy. That's one of the reasons why some go off their medications on weekends or over vacation.

Be sure to invite your parents into doing some real research into prescription medication. Some have side effects such as a "fuzziness," or unclear thinking, or fogginess and confusion. Some make it hard for you to sleep at night and to eat as much food as you did before. Some may even result in some added frustration and irritability. Keep in mind that, among other things, nutrients and rest assist your body and brain in their optimal functioning.

This is a real conversation to have with your parents and your doctor. Keep in mind, you are an individual, and what seems to work on everyone else may or may not be the best solution for you. For some of my clients, herbs and supplements have really helped them. It needs to be an ongoing process and dialogue with yourself, your parents, and other professionals to find your best solution(s).

Please do not consider medication as a stopping point. Continual practice and development of your attentiveness and awareness of your emotional state must be a part of your plan. The rest of this book contains exercises that help you do just that. Medications do not necessarily improve your brain's own independent development of working memory. Only *you* can do that. Remember that working memory is the key player in all of your executive functions. **Most grades have so little to do with your intellect and so much to do with your ability to plan and organize and simply turn stuff in on time.** Medication may give you an added oomph to do those things, but it doesn't increase your brain's natural capacity to build its own working memory skills. In other words, medication works from the outside in, and not the inside out. It should not really be considered as the sole method for improvement; your brain still needs its own unique combination of development tools. Everyone is different, and the same solution does not work best for all.

Ask your parents to do thorough research and to ask lots of questions to find the best answer for you and your individual needs. Keep an open mind. Be willing to try different options, natural alternatives, therapies, and systems and you will find the right combination of what works just for you. Several of my clients opt out of medication and choose redox signaling molecules, essential oils, herbs, or supplements. These, in combination with the other tools in this book, have led to some incredible learning and living transformations.

Whatever you and your family decide, maintain an open dialogue about changes you observe and how things are going. No one pill, prescription or not, will be the solution to all of your problems. **Your best "medicine" is to learn new behaviors and means of self-empowerment that honor your unique learning style.**

Keep in mind that you are in a state of constant flux, and your solutions will need to change along with you.

My job is to provide you insights and suggestions to new things that may help you along your journey, to provide tools for transformation.

Part 2 of this book offers several uniquely different tools that you can use, try out, and combine to develop your own learning empowerment plan. Most will be new to you, and may be weirdly different than things you already know. Not everything is going to work for everyone, but being aware of these tools can help you find your right combination of solutions. **Pick and choose what does work and then switch it up as needed.** I've helped many a student perform his or her best by using these tools. So, do enjoy and feel free to use these as a launchpad. Adapt these tools to your own needs and preferences so you can create your own success!

Part 2:

Chapter 5:

Expand Your Capacity

Fortunately, there exists an abundance of new techniques and tools out there to help you. I will dedicate the rest of this book to helping you discover some of those options and choose the right tools for you. Most of these you will be able to pick up and use immediately on your own, without extra money or adult supervision. Some of them cost money or require parental involvement. The good news is that there is plenty to choose from, and you get to decide what's best for you.

One really great tool is a working memory program that challenges you on working memory tasks. This, over time, **builds your capacity to hold onto more pieces of information**, which allows you to strengthen the links between them and form a working chain of information. Imagine solving problems with this newer, stronger piece of equipment. It is like giving you a larger and larger capacity to hold and manipulate information each time you use it so you can work more efficiently, accomplishing more work in less time, and remember details and stay on task.

What would an expanded working memory capacity mean for you? The benefits are so many: problem-solving, planning, and organization all improve. **Just imagine what life would look like with all of that--better decisions, less stress, more free time, and improved confidence.**

Some working memory experts have designed specially made training programs just to grow your working memory capacity. Do your research and talk with a providing professional to know which one is right for you. Cogmed Working Memory Training (CWMT), for instance, is one of the strongest tools available for working memory intervention. It does require parental involvement. If you are interested, be sure to have your parents ask your potential local provider for a trial link so you know what it's like. You can explore it more at *my.cogmed.com*. Be sure to have your parents check it out, especially the research. They can consult a professional provider in your area and ask questions.

Build some of your own working memory challenges by requiring yourself to remember as many items on a list as possible, following as many steps as possible in a set of directions, or repeating a series of numbers (like a phone number) backwards. As you see street names, license plates, or recipes, see how many pieces you can hold onto at one time. Then push yourself to add just one more. Try it both forward and in reverse. If you play video games, get the ones that build on multiple previous steps to attain your goals.

Above all, use what you now know about working memory to help you study, read, solve problems, and take tests.

You now know that the smaller the working memory load, the greater the chances of processing and assimilating new information. Break memory tasks into one, two, or three pieces at a time. As you get stronger, challenge yourself to do four and five at a time, building all the way up to seven, and maybe eight. This alone increases your capacity.

If solving a problem, do only a small part first, then eventually to add another step at a time until you can do three to four steps in a sequence. Start small and then build up.

When reading, skim first and get the gist, then add another layer of depth, and finally do a full read for the whole picture. Each pass through the material allows for more bits of information to stick to each other, to form meaning and to make sense in your brain. When things make sense, they stick! Yes, you are reading it at least three times, but it is now sticking. Knowing how to use what you now know about working memory makes all the difference.

I've literally seen students spend a whole hour reading a page and then retain none of it. By allowing yourself to move forward, gaining a bit more each time, you actually accomplish and retain more in less time. Upon completion, stop, recall, and write down three things you remember from what you read. Revisit what you wrote down each day, bringing it to memory, and you'll be three steps ahead for your next assessment.

You're already getting stronger!

Chapter 6:

Let's Talk About Stress, Baby!

I always start my clients on **life skills before organization and study skills.** Why? Because decreased anxiety and stress puts you in a better mindset and lays the groundwork for all your other needs. Do this first. Even if you don't think you have test anxiety, building resilience provides necessary skills for future success.

Increased stress almost always goes along with any kind of difficulty in school or any learning challenge. When your information linking is not as strong as the rest of your brain, **you actually have to work harder, do more steps, and repeat previous steps more often. This adds more to your working memory load, and increases what you have to process.** That's right. So, working memory capacity is already reduced, but you have to add even more steps to your processing. Now that's super-difficult.

If anyone tells you that you are not working hard enough, they are probably mistaken. Please feel free to tell them I said so. **You actually have to work harder than your focus-typical peers to accomplish tasks.** Think of a waiter having to run back and forth to the kitchen many, many times to gather items he knows he needs, but that didn't fit on the tray. His table of customers is getting mad because their food is getting cold, and they are not all getting their meal at the same time due to his need to make multiple trips.

Now imagine his reaction to getting a smaller tip, even though he worked more than twice as hard as his fellow waiters. Bummer. And then imagine his boss telling him he just needs to work a little harder, or even carry two trays at a time. Double bummer.

This would be frustrating for the waiter, and it's the same with school. If you struggle with school work, chances are high that you readily experience mental fatigue, and just like that waiter, your brain is carrying many trays of information back and forth and can therefore fatigue quickly. Among other things, a rapid fatigue rate can wear you down, raise the difficulty level of your task, and cause more stress. Stress can manifest in many different forms. My clients typically express high levels of anxiety, depression, overwhelm, frustration, and even anger, especially with regards to school or tasks.

Learning is not merely an intellectual process; it is also an emotional one. When emotions such as panic, worry, fear, frustration, and anger show up as a result of having difficulty, learning can trigger the production of cortisol and other stress chemicals in the body. These chemicals do serve a real-life purpose, and a good one at that. The body needs these when we are facing a life-threatening situation--you know, like being attacked by a bear. This can be a good thing if we need to defend ourselves (fight) or run for our lives (flight).

We all know that tests and even some assignments are not bears, but sometimes they threaten us. They may threaten our perception of our own intelligence or even self-worth. They may threaten how we measure up to our classmates and if we please (or don't please) our parents. If you have ever had a bad experience with a test before, guess what? Your brain just might be patterned to register that negative experience each and every time you see a test, or maybe even at the mere mention of a test. That fear is not your truth. You actually love to demonstrate what you know.

Now that we understand why these feelings arise, what can we do about it?

Fortunately there are tools out there to help us recognize and process our stressors, and even transform stress into productivity.

One very practical method for lowering stress is to apply some HeartMath® steps.

HeartMath® is a system of learning to bring your heart rate variability into a healthy balance, so you are better able to respond to stressors. A HeartMath® coach can help you do this. You can even start on your own with these first simple steps:

1. Focus on the area of the heart.
2. Breathe into your heart, as if you were simply breathing in and out of your heart space.

This alone is enough to get you started toward lowering a stressful response. Further coaching can help you manage your stress levels and give you tools to use your heart rate variability as a measure to increase resilience and problem-solving ability, specifically your natural or intuitive problem-solving ability. It paves the way for clearer thinking and better performance in tasks and life. You can find HeartMath® resources, such as tools and a coach on their website: *www.heartmath.com*.

For most of my clients, HeartMath® offers immediate relief and can be developed into a powerful personal practice. I usually encourage my clients' parents to practice HeartMath® along with my clients. Parents can learn more by reading *The HeartMath Solution: The Institute of HeartMath's Revolutionary Program for Engaging the Power of the Heart's Intelligence* (2000) by Doc Lew Childre and Howard Martin. It's always best for parents to practice alongside their children, because that way it improves overall interaction and leads to problem-solving rather than blame.

Another very powerful tool is The LifeLine Technique®.

Over time, stress and negative reactions prevent us from moving forward and being the successful people we want to be. Why is this? It's not like you woke up and said, "I think I want to sabotage all my efforts today, and not only that, I want to be totally stressed out, worried, and frustrated. In fact, I think I'll just choose to forget that information I studied for today's test." You'd never do that, right? In the words of Dr. Darren Weissman, founder of The LifeLine Technique®, "What is not a choice or an action is a reaction." So if you didn't choose all this, then it's a reaction. A reaction is a part of you that responds automatically, without your thinking about it--like a reflex to protect you. If, due to a past negative experience, a learning situation feels unsafe (a teacher or peer may have ridiculed you, for example, or you simply felt stupid or not good enough), it's enough to trigger a reaction. Chances are, you do not even remember that original situation or even recognize that you're being triggered or acting out of fear.

I've been working with students for several years, and the one thing I can assure you of is this: **No student ever consciously chooses to fail**. Some might get burned out or even self-sabotage due to negative associations and bad experiences or processing challenges, but that's not really a conscious choice--it's more like a reaction, and one you wouldn't choose.

You'd never choose to feel this test anxiety, this stress, this pressure, not to mention how it makes you feel in your body. This means that it happens automatically and that you're not choosing it. The Lifeline Technique® teaches you how to choose what you do want, to set an intention for yourself in a way that sticks, and it makes a huge difference.

Dr. Darren has developed an amazing way to have you connect to the present moment and then observe your symptoms and stressors in present time. Because you can't move forward until you acknowledge what's going on in the present. Once you've observed the stressors, there's a huge question, a "million dollar" question: Would you ever choose to create your day, your life with all those symptoms and stressors? Your answer is a very strong no, in fact, an emphatic, "Heck no!"

If you take a LifeLine Ignite class or work with a Certified LifeLine Practitioner, you learn to set a heart-based intention, once that you would choose, and seal that intention in. Over time, usually about five sessions, you create new patterns for yourself that result in your ability to create what you want rather than react to whatever life seems to throw at you. Once you learn the tools, it is an ongoing process that you use to create your life.

Embracing learning with intention is a total game-changer. It puts you in control as a learner. Imagine creating your day according to your intention as opposed to waiting to see what is going to happen next and then reacting to it. You can literally build your own world instead of waiting around for things to happen. I've worked with many students in The LifeLine Technique®, and they leave feeling as they would choose to feel: confident and empowered.

The Lifeline Technique® treats all symptoms and stressors as portals--opportunities for making your life better. Imagine converting stress into more of what you want out of life--that's what it does. Consider having a LifeLine session with a Certified LifeLine Practitioner (CLP), or doing a LifeLine Ignite course with your parents. Over time, the Ignite process can be done very quickly, and it becomes an awesome life hack. It will help your parents too. **Parents don't choose to be anxious, angry, worried, or frustrated--they're just reacting in the best and only ways they know how. Adults are just more experienced subconscious reactors because they've spent more time in their reactive patterns, ones they probably wouldn't choose.** Just because adults are older and have more responsibility and earn money doesn't mean they're perfect. Trust me, if they knew better, they'd do better.

Besides creating a mindset more like what you would choose for yourself, The Lifeline Technique® can also improve your brain function. It includes techniques that help you get present and improve your processing ability by developing your visual, kinesthetic, and auditory processing, which helps out your problem-solving abilities in a holistic way. How awesome is that??

You can find resources, classes and practitioners for The LifeLine Technique® by visiting *www.thelifelinecenter.com*.

HeartMath® and The LifeLine Technique® can really help you improve your performance in life and at school. Their websites can help you get in touch with a coach to teach you some extremely effective steps. These can help you to solve problems more easily, which really comes in handy in not only test and homework situations, but in ALL situations.

You also might want to consider talk therapy to learn to recognize your responses and decide what to do about them. Cognitive Behavioral Therapy and Dialectical Behavior Therapy are useful tools you can use with a trained therapist. Filling out a Cognitive Behavior Therapy Chart can help you to see your situation differently. Examples look something like this:

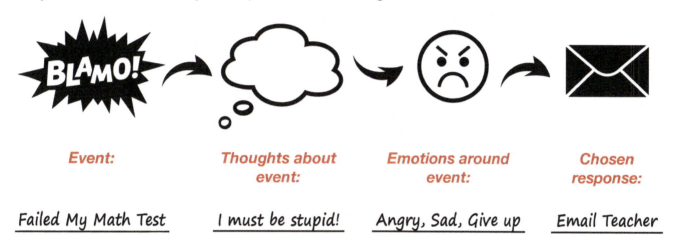

Event:	Thoughts about event:	Emotions around event:	Chosen response:
Failed My Math Test	I must be stupid!	Angry, Sad, Give up	Email Teacher

Lastly, but certainly not least, meditation offers several benefits, including improved focus, resilience, and stress relief. If it is hard to sit still, it may feel difficult at first. **If you do struggle to sit still, it is a strong indicator that building a meditation practice will benefit you.** You can start small, very, very small, even for less than a minute, and eventually build to five to ten to fifteen minutes. Find the meditation style that works best for you, like mindfulness meditation or transcendental meditation. If you feel uncertain, guided meditation is a great way to start out. There are plenty to sample online. As with everything else, find one that pleases you. If you can't find any that you like, sample a Yoga Nidra (rest) recording. It's okay if you fall asleep, because your brain will still reap the benefits of brain balance, increased interconnectivity, and relaxation, all of which improve task performance. Be sure to listen to samples first, and make sure that the voice is one that relaxes you. Everyone is different and has different preferences. There is one out there just for you.

Let's sum up:

Negative emotions in the form of stress can jumble your brain's ability to process information. There is no way to avoid stress--the key is learning how to use it.

If not managed, perceptions that cause stress can lead to reactions and more negative emotions--which makes it even harder to process information, problem solve, and get stuff done, kind of like a bad hamster wheel.

There are several tools, such as those listed above, that can help convert a negative into a positive--something that you would choose for yourself.

In a sense, **it's a gift to have these struggles**. If you use them properly, they can lead to greater personal development. Again, it's a matter of what feels best for you, so choose your tools for transformation accordingly and investigate more on your own. Most of us would rather have big results fast, which is why the immediate and applicable skills in this chapter tend to create successful outcomes early on. Whatever you choose, stick with it and allow it to generate new pathways in your brain and body. Your investment in stress reduction will definitely pay off in life and school improvements, big time!

Chapter 7:

Be About It!

So far we have discussed some possibilities for improving your brain's capacity: increasing resilience with HeartMath® skills; giving your working memory a structured workout; and working with a coach are all very effective means to help you work more efficiently, so you get more work done in less time.

Most of those involve getting an adult to help you. So what are some things you can do on your own? I thought you'd never ask!

The nice thing about the following practices is that you can do them any time and they cost nothing. They bear the potential to empower you.

Are you ready? Here you go… the world is at your fingertips!

1. Positive Visualization

Imagine yourself improving in any area: studying well, taking notes, taking a test with ease and confidence. Try this example on for size:

Picture yourself seated for your next test. You have taken good notes and reviewed your notes daily. You prepared by making yourself a practice test. You are calm and confident knowing that you have this opportunity to demonstrate your hard work and knowledge. Picture yourself going through the test and reading each question thoroughly and answering thoughtfully. You may even picture yourself using your HeartMath® skills during the test. Really put yourself in the situation as you visualize this! Feel your emotions, hear the sound in the classroom, feel yourself at the desk. Absorb this input with a positive feeling. Here's the best brain-hack ever: your brain doesn't know the difference between a real and an imagined experience. By doing these exercises, **you are actually building a bank of positive emotion, chemicals, and feedback for your brain that help it perform at its best.**

Not everyone will form a picture right away; some of you are stronger at sensing. It doesn't matter. Just put yourself through the experience in your imagination and add a positive feeling.

This is no hocus pocus. Your brain simply reacts to an imagined experience as if it were real. Try it out for yourself right now. Imagine sucking on a nice, freshly cut lemon wedge. The salivary response is already acting *as if* you really were. That's right! The same way you can imagine a negative experience and get nervous or agitated, you can just as easily imagine a positive one and get productive. You can actually build up the capacity to do this by frequently imagining positive outcomes in your mind. See them, feel them, hear them. Need to talk to your teacher or give a class presentation? Allow yourself to experience it going well several times beforehand. The more you "experience" positive outcomes, the more you prime your brain to produce positive feelings and thus create a stronger mindset.

2. Affirmations

Say positive statements aloud to yourself. For bonus points, say them into a mirror and write them down and post them all around you: on your mirror, where you study, where you eat, on your laptop, wherever you think best. As you say them, practice the visualization process above. This will reinforce their transformative effect. Try some or all of these:

Every day, I am learning more and more.

I enjoy learning new things.

Every day, learning to focus becomes easier and easier for me.

- I have laser-like focus on this task.
- I do my hardest task first.
- I am accomplished.
- I stop and summarize what I have just read.
- I love finishing my tasks with plenty of time left.
- I actively prepare for tests and quizzes.
- I quiz myself daily on each new section of material.
- I enjoy my new skills and I practice them daily.
- I take notes that are fun and easy to review.
- Frequent review makes it fun and easy for me to study.
- I am calm and relaxed. I think clearly.
- Change is good. I am willing to change.
- Each moment is a new opportunity to be my best self.

3. "Hypnosis" and "Self-hypnosis"

Contrary to popular belief, hypnosis is not much more than a combination of visualization and affirmations. The only difference is that hypnosis works with your brain in an Alpha state. Before you get all weirded out—let me explain. The Alpha state is the one right below normal brain operations (otherwise known as the Beta state). The Alpha state is just a greater degree of relaxation. You actually experience this state daily, whether you are aware of it or not. It's what happens when you are completely absorbed in something that relaxes you. If you play video games, read books, or draw, then you have experienced this relaxed brain state. It kind of removes you from everyday reality, but only slightly. You can come back out into normal operations at any given time.

A hypnosis recording or a hypnotist might put you in Alpha state by asking you to imagine yourself in your favorite surroundings, like the beach, or in a peaceful meadow. This is to relax you. Then suggestions about focus and studying become more powerful because you aren't busy analyzing the positive suggestions or giving yourself reasons to doubt them.

Chapter 8:

Let Your Fingers Do the Talking

And no, I'm not talking about flashing the middle finger.

An effective use of your fingers is to apply your fingers to your meridians.

A meridian is an invisible pathway in your body that carries energy through every part of you. Touching just two (or more) fingers to your thumb unleashes some powerful internal motivation.

Versions of tapping on meridian (emotional channel) points are powerful ways to transform your life or learning experience. They are cost-free and pain-free and they can give you a huge boost, especially before you sit down to study or do homework. If you are overwhelmed and procrastinate a lot, chances are that this will work for you. I've had several clients, adults and children alike, respond immediately to this approach. It's short, it's easy, and it's even fun. Until you get the hang of it, it's best to work with a certified professional in person, or even via video (try looking online) or by using pre-written scripts.

Tapping on the meridians in a certain sequence releases trapped patterns that are stored in the body. Then the freedom kicks in. Once the patterns are acknowledged and released, you are free to choose a new pattern.

It's amazing how much your focus and concentration improve when you address stress, overwhelm, and self-sabotage patterns such as procrastination. For several reasons, those who have ADHD often experience accompanying conditions like depression, anxiety, overwhelm, feeling not-good-enough, etc. These conditions spark a rise in stress hormones, and, as you now know, further cloud your ability to focus and think clearly.

Try this sample tapping script for homework and see how it works.

First, rate your degree of not liking or not wanting to start your work. Rate it on a scale of 1-10 with 1 being not really averse to it, and 10 being it's a great big huge frickin' deal to get going. Write that number down.

Now you're ready to start tapping. Using all your fingers and your thumb, tap on the following points according to the following diagram while repeating the suggested statements aloud.

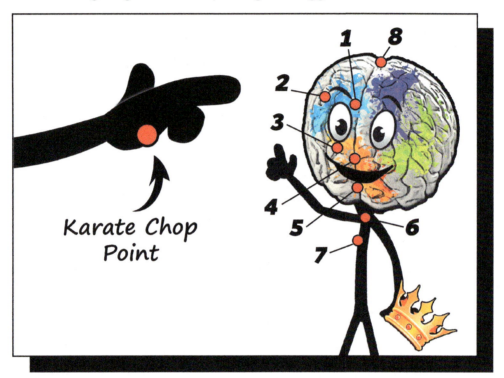

Tapping the **Karate Chop point,** repeat:

> "Even though I have so much to do and it's hard for me to focus, I love, appreciate, and accept myself."

> "Even though focusing is hard for me and I have difficulty doing my work, I love, appreciate, and accept myself."

> "Even though this work is definitely hard and it takes me longer to do it, I deeply love, appreciate, and accept myself."

1: **Inner brow:** This work is so hard, so hard.

2: **Outer brow:** I have trouble focusing

3: **Under eye**: It's hard to sit still and do it. So hard!

4: **Under nose**: Nobody gets this! Nobody!

5: **Between chin and lower lip:** I get stuck on problems. Very stuck.

6: **Collarbone:** I don't know what my teacher wants.

7: **Below armpit:** I forget how we do this. OMG! WTFrick do I do?

8: **Top of head:** What if I do just one step and then see where I go?

1: **Inner brow:** What if I set a time for just ten minutes? I can do this for ten minutes.

2: **Outer brow:** Yes. I can put ten minutes in.

3: **Under eye:** And see where it goes.

4: **Under nose:** And then ask for help.

5: **Between chin and lower lip:** Heck, I can move on to something else, even if just for ten minutes.

6: **Collarbone:** I can work for ten minutes. I can do that.

7: **Under armpit:** Okay, I'm going to move forward, give this a try, and see what happens.

8: **Top of head:** I can do this.

Stop and rate the intensity of your negativity toward your schoolwork.

What was the intensity rating before you began?

What is it now? If it's **above a 5, run the script again starting at the top of script where it begins at the inner brow point**.

Chapter 9:

Fuel Your Brain!

BRAINS OPERATE AT THEIR BEST WHEN FED PROPER PROTEINS AND FATS AND CLEAN, PURE WATER.

Just as all of your muscles are made of cells that have needs like nutrients and oxygen, your brain is made of cells that need those same things. Think about it: cells are cells. You wouldn't let the cells in your muscles and organs starve and weaken, so you should do the same things to strengthen your brain cells that you would for your muscles. Brains operate at their best when fed proper proteins and fats and clean, pure water.

Protein is essential to maintain your focus. The brain needs and utilizes proteins the same way your muscles do—as building blocks. When your brain is operating, it needs to build more connections and pathways, which requires cellular production. Think of protein as the building blocks for attaining more strength and power in the brain. Protein-rich foods include meats, eggs, dairy, legumes (bean-like veggies), nuts, and seeds. Some grains, like oats and quinoa (okay, so quinoa really is a seed, not a grain) are also high in protein.

Fats, the good kind, are like liquid gold for the brain. They help keep everything running smoothly. The best fats are Omega-3s. Omega-3s can be found in fish oil, but if you prefer vegetarian sources for your Omega-3s, there are even better ones for you. It turns out that fish derive their omegas from the algae that they eat, so if you don't like fish, go straight to the source—algae oils!

The right kinds of carbs, complex carbs, are also good for the brain. Whole grains, vegetables, and fruits give you and your brain energy to stay active and get stuff done. They're like the fuel you and your brain need to keep going. Many people whom I work with are gluten-sensitive—it means that their bodies do not properly break down glutinous substances found in some oats, rye, wheat, and barley. If you are gluten-sensitive, stick with gluten-free oats, brown rice, quinoa (not really a grain but used as one), and other gluten-free foods.

It's always a good idea to balance out proteins, fats, and carbs so that you and your brain can operate optimally. You don't want all energy and no strength/stamina, and you don't want all strength with no energy, and you certainly **do** want the oils to deliver stuff where it needs to go. Eat meals and choose snacks that are balanced. The United States Department of Agriculture (USDA) has a diagram of what they recommend as a balanced meal on their website at *www.choosemyplate.gov*. There are also plenty of guidelines there for choosing food and balancing your meals. Avoid the dairy if it's not for you, and opt for plant-based milks like hemp, almond, coconut, and flax.

Lastly and most importantly, hydrate, hydrate, hydrate! For every 50 pounds you weigh, you should drink four cups of water every day. Most of us lack sufficient hydration for our brains and bodies to function optimally. The body delivers messages to us through symptoms. Some of the symptoms of not having enough water in your body are irritability, fatigue, muscle cramping, and--get this--inability to focus! If you're feeling fuzzy, ask yourself when you last had water.

Consuming enough water--clean, pure, non-carbonated water--is perhaps the most important thing you do for yourself all day.

Most of us struggle with water consumption for two reasons:

1. We tend to be forgetful. One of your new working memory exercises might be to remember your water. We struggle with remembering things like this because we are easily distracted and can get carried away and lose track of time, so it might help to get one of those water reminder apps on your phone. I can tell you from experience that remembering to carry our water with us is a real chore. Set an evening reminder on your phone that tells you to fill and pack your water bottle. Your body and your brain will thank you for it.

2. We fill ourselves with other beverages--some of which deplete us and flush even more fluids out of the body. Your sodas, diet sodas, and favorite coffee drinks do just that. Furthermore, the sugar in your sodas might make you feel good at first, and you may even crave that sensation, but it is seriously messing with your blood sugar, metabolism, and ability to concentrate. Many of my clients feel an immediate change when they shift to drinking the right amount of plain water.

The brain not only likes water, it depends on that water to function properly. A dry brain is an unhappy brain. The brain is not a cactus, and cannot go long periods of time without proper hydration.

Chapter 10:

Move Your Body!

Countless studies have shown the benefits of physical exercise on the brain. Exercise lowers stress levels and gets the motor cortex to engage with your pre-frontal cortex, the part where you do all of your organizing, foresight, structuring, and planning. Think about running outside, for instance. All of your senses have to be engaged and communicating together. You must be aware of what is underneath your feet, the path that lies ahead, and the perimeter. You need to look ahead for downed branches, animals, or other runners. You are aware of physical sensations at the same time you're making mental calculations. In the meanwhile your serotonin and dopamine levels are getting a huge boost. This is excellent practice for staying engaged and aware of what is going on around you at all times, simultaneously. Having a feel-good chemical already charged in your body provides the added benefit of increased memory and processing ability. This is great for your brain! It's like an internal tango happening where your brain and body learn to cooperate. Yes!

I encourage my clients to get 20-30 minutes of moderate-to-intense activity in the morning before engaging in school-related tasks. Make sure it is an activity that you enjoy naturally, like maybe running, bouncing, biking, swimming, or yoga--the flowing kind, not necessarily the sit-and-stretch kind. I especially recommend "cross-crawling" activities where you are moving opposite arms and legs together, as if you were crawling. Swimming and some yoga and dance are awesome examples of this. **Cross-crawling encourages the right and left hemispheres of the brain to interact together, leading to whole-brain engagement, and therefore better memory and focus.**

You were not designed to sit all day, nor should you! Consider fidget-friendly gadgets and furniture that allow you to move and engage while thinking. The working memory part of your brain, while doing its problem-solving and processing, usually likes a motor stimulant, or movement to help it work better and function more naturally. So the more you move, the better you think, boo!

I must admit, I roll my eyes (really, I do!) when parents and teachers tell me that they train you to sit still and not fidget. Really?! This is the opposite of what we want. **Please fidget.** Yes, take this to your parents and teachers and show them what I said. In fact, I want you to purchase a fidget (a toy you can squeeze or manipulate with your hands while working) for yourself and have one at your desk, especially at home. Do not, however, bring a throwable fidget to school. No explanation required.

I also like standing desks, wiggle chairs, balance ball chairs, and and bike desks for my clients. It's always best to "try before you buy" so you can find what's best for you.

There, so now you have my permission. Fidget away! And don't forget to work in some moderate-to-intense exercise early in the day.

Chapter 11:

Be Your Own Best Advocate!

I've heard from many a student that their teacher "hates" them. Hate is a strong word and carries a heavy emotional weight. It can feel like rejection, hopelessness, anger, resentment, shame, and guilt--for both teacher and student. Teachers seldom "hate" students. The most likely scenario is that they misunderstand, or view the student through a lens of misperception based on their own background and experiences. They might perceive an unwillingness or lack of respect that is simply your need to get up and fidget, or need for better homework instructions.

I have a secret for you: you are good enough and you are worthy of support. Just because you learn differently doesn't mean you are a burden or an extra weight on anybody. It simply means the adults in your life need more information. Your parents are usually good at delivering that information, but sometimes it comes best from you. When the adults in your life are better-equipped with information, they do a better job of adulting.

It can sometimes be intimidating to approach a teacher, especially if you are doing poorly and you think that your teacher "hates" you. In most cases, your teacher doesn't hate you. Sometimes he or she needs to understand a little more. Just like you, and me, and your parents, if your teacher could do better, she would. Equipping her with what you now know about yourself is a strong entryway to improved communication.

Here is a sample letter you could write to a teacher. Feel free to adjust to suit your own needs.

Dear _____,

My name is _____. I've attached this picture of me for you.

As we start our learning journey together, there are a few things you might want to know about me:

First of all, I love _____. I also love learning, but some things might be difficult for me.

For instance, when I "drift off" and look out the window or stare for long periods of time, I really don't mean to. It would really help me if you could walk by and place a hand on my desk or on my materials as a reminder to "come back" that doesn't call attention to the whole class.

If I forget my homework or leave it at home, you should know that I really did forget. You see, things don't stick in my brain the way they do with neurotypical students. Keeping all due dates and instructions in writing really helps me out a lot.

I also lose a lot of papers. Sorry. Handing out whole sheets with holes already punched and making sure we all have time to place them in the proper folders and binders increases the chances that I will be able to find a paper when I need it for homework or to study. But, just in case, can you post an extra copy online? Thanks.

Homework is hard for me for several reasons. I can't always remember the explanations and instructions that you give in class, so it takes extra time to try to research those (again, if they're posted online, extra thanks!). I also have difficulty linking together pieces of information for problem solving. If I get too many pieces of information to hold onto all at once, I lose track and have to start all over again. This takes extra time as I am constantly retracing my steps. This means that my brain gets tired faster and that I get frustrated and burned out easily. The frustration makes my brain work less efficiently, which makes everything even harder! Sometimes I experience tears over this and want to give up.

If homework gets repeatedly hard, like I just described above, I assume it's always going to cause me tears and frustration, so it becomes harder and harder to sit down and do it. It's called a negative memory, and it's stuck in my brain patterning. It sometimes gets hard for me to ask you for help, because I feel like I should know how to start and continue. I don't like to show you just how stuck I really am. I'm afraid you might think I'm stupid, or that you might yell at me for not paying attention.

I guess the best thing we can work on together is our system of communication. Frequent feedback to direct me, or redirect me, would really help. I am more than happy to send you a screenshot or image of where I am stuck and the steps I have already taken. If that does not work for you, is there a step-by-step website you prefer I consult? Or do you make your own tutorial videos? Please let me know and we will work together. Thank you!

Another thing. If I fidget, squirm, or get out of my seat a lot, it means my body needs to move. When my brain gets activated and I start solving problems using my working memory skills, my body needs to move too, so it can help my brain move along. It's like when one part gets animated, my motor cortex jumps in as a co-stimulant to help me think better. Many have tried to get me to stop doing this, but it's best if you help me figure out a way to move quietly with the use of a fidget toy or chair cushion that allows me to wiggle without too much distraction. At home I might even use a stability ball or bike desk.

I am a really good kid, and you're a really good teacher. Let's keep talking about helping each other out!

Thank you,

_____

Chapter 12:

Be Your Own Expert!

Okay, so I have given you many ways to make school less "sucky." The most powerful thing you can do, boo, is to stay informed. Do not settle for what all the adults tell you. They mean well, but they don't know everything. Trust me. So, the best thing you can do for yourself is to get to know your own brain and body and how it all works together.

Experts say that **you are more likely to stick with solutions you come up with on your own.** Besides, it changes the conversation. Instead of your parents and teachers telling you what you are doing wrong, you are guiding them to be better mentors.

Becoming more informed might entail some reading or joining a Facebook page. You can start by liking my Facebook page, **I Heart Learning, llc** (*www.facebook.com/iheart2learn*). ADDitude magazine (*www.additudemag.com*) is also an excellent resource for all the latest information on study skills, exercise suggestions, and other helpful topics. Knowing the latest information is always helpful. So many new technologies and guidelines are popping up all the time. Look up fidget tools, large timers, standing desks, vitamins, and nutritional recommendations for starters!

Try simply googling the topic you're struggling with. For example, try "how do I get better at reading," "cellular respiration," "how to solve a linear equation," "tips for focus," or even, "how to stay interested when the teacher/topic is boring."

Create or join a social media page for study tips or note-taking. There are some genius hacks out there. Want to know why? Because you're not the only one who has struggled. Others have too, and they've found solutions. Save yourself some time by using what they've learned, and hey, who knows? Maybe you'll have something to share with others.

So, you're saying, "You already know how hard it is for me to read, focus, and process information, and you're asking me to read?!"

You bet I am. I wouldn't be a very good coach if I did not empower you.

Chapter 13:

Rev-Up Your Reading!

Reading might be difficult because you have to process information and comprehend it at the same time, and you're expected to remember what you've read. These all engage the same functions of your brain and are difficult for any one of us to do all at once.

Furthermore, traditional reading, one word at a time, fatigues the brain, slows you down, overwhelms the working memory, and reduces the chances of processing and storing what you've read as useable chunks of information.

Your best option, then, is to actively speed the process up. I like to refer to my process as "non-reading," and by "non-reading" I mean processing the information first, then looking at the words. What you "non-read" will make a whole lot more sense and it will be easier on your brain. If you can combine it with some skillful note-taking, then better retention is a natural consequence. Studying the material will be a breeze because you'll already know and remember it.

Here's some help: use my reading plan! It breaks down the steps for you so you can first process, then comprehend, and then link stuff together.

Let's give it a try. Go ahead! Look up an article or grab a chapter of your textbook and then come back.

Okay, if you made it back right away, great job. If you got distracted and walked away or got "lost" for a bit, no worries, my partner, it's all part of the territory!

Are you ready? Let's go.

First things first.

Step one: Feel a positive emotion in your heart center, like feeling like you've already completed this assignment, and you have retained the information gathered from your reading!

Step two: Spend just one minute and allow your eyes to scan the pages you've selected. Pick out 4-5 words per page that you think might be important. Have you ever been to the beach? It's my favorite place! Have you ever seen a pelican or a seagull hover over the water and dive straight down to grab up a fish? Well, you can be like that seabird, but you are fishing for words instead. Don't pick out just any word, pick out the best, most informative, and even most fun words you can find!

Step three: Make some guesses. Based on your juicy words, piece together what you think the reading might be about.

Step four: Read just enough to see if you are right. Stop there.

Step five: Set a timer. Start it at three minutes. **Read for only three minutes. STOP! Summarize to yourself what you just read.** If this is for school, write it down.(Now you've also taken notes!) That's it. With practice you will work your way up to five and eventually to ten to even twenty minutes of sustained reading time. Start small at first, then build your way up. Be sure to summarize after each reading segment. You can use a pencil right in your book or keep separate reading notes in a notebook.

Preparing for your next test or quiz will be a snap.

As you find articles about your particular learning style, don't just sit there, do something! Start your own social networking group. Share that info. You might want to invite your parents, teachers, and peers to join. You build the group and share as you'd like it to stay. It can be just a group of friends, but remember, informed adults are better adults, so let them know what you have found!

Chapter 14:

Super-Size Your Results

How many times have you been told to "study" more? **"Study" is a bad word in my book.** Too often students do exactly what they are told to do. You sit down to "study," meaning that you examine the information before you, staring at the page. After some eyeball time, you have re-examined the material and consider it "studied." You may even have reread your previous assignments.

In a sense, you are right, if to study means to examine and observe. You walk away with a stronger understanding of the material and are amazed that your test, usually on the following day, does not reflect your strenuous observation efforts.

This would be just fine if, on the assessment (a word teachers use for things like quizzes and tests), you were asked to observe and understand the material. Usually, however, you are asked to do more on an assessment. Most assessments ask you to manipulate and reproduce what you have learned, not simply observe it. Here are some questions to ask yourself to determine your own readiness for an assessment.

1. Can I reproduce the material (formulas, facts, data, structure, etc.) without support?
2. Can I explain the concepts to another person in a clear and concise way?
3. Can I use the information given to answer hypothetical scenarios, such as, "what if _____ were to happen?"

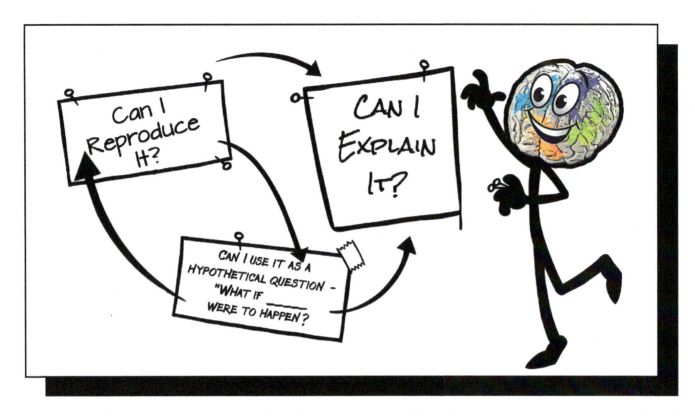

If your answer to these questions is "Yes," congratulations! You just need to review and practice. If the answer is "No," "Not quite," "Not completely," or "Not yet," you have an awesome opportunity to empower yourself. **By challenging yourself to engage more actively with your materials, you set yourself up for success**.

What are some ways to achieve active review habits? For each of us, the best ways vary. Try some of the suggestions below, or apply some creative genius to come up with some of your own.

1. Cover up your notes, diagrams, and pages and reproduce what you already know. Leave blank spaces for what you don't know. If you really want to amp up your grades, do this daily with each new day's material. This way you are never really "studying" in that traditional sense of trying to cram it all in at once. Daily reframing and applying recently acquired material drastically improves retention and performance on tests and quizzes.
2. Create your own test or quiz. Place yourself in the mindset of the test-maker. Once you are aware of a teacher's style, you can learn to repeat that on your own and follow their model.

3. Change up your notes into a visual. Look up some images of visual note-taking on the internet or social media for inspiration. Keep a running vision board, electronic or paper with ideas for studying. If an image appeals to you, it increases the likelihood for your own absorption and application of a new technique. You may even want to pin some ideas and share a board of your own.
4. Make up a *mnemonic*, or memory device for lists or formulas. This might look like taking the first letter of every word in a list and making a silly sentence, such as King Phillip Came Over From Greece Swimming in place of Kingdom, Phylum, Class, Order, Family Genus, Species. Alternately, take a formula and make it into a word.
5. On a daily basis, recall and reproduce what happened in class. Try to sum it up in a word or two, like photosynthesis, balancing equations, subject-verb agreement, or *la ropa*.
6. Figure out your strengths and find a practice that matches your strengths. Some students like to see, some like to hear, and some prefer to move. Work with what you like to do. Repeat material while walking or bouncing a ball, make up a song, draw a diagram, or create a poster.

Studying gets a bad rap because, unless you know how to do it, it can be a waste of time and energy. If you've had bad experiences studying, it's not your fault. Consider it a sign that you need to find a way to fire up that creative side and make your review practices more active and engaging. You can do it!

Chapter 15:

Get a Coach!

So, it turns out I saved the best for last. I have read countless books and articles on how to get organized and stop procrastinating and study better. In these, I have found many sound pieces of advice that I have tried out. But I have yet to find that one book or that one system that works for everybody. If I had, I would not have written this book for your sweet self! I would have just said, "Hey, go read so-and-so." That would not have made for a very interesting book, would it?

Here are a few of my top tips I share with students:

1. **Set a timer.** If it's hard to get started on homework, a project, or on cleaning up your room, set a timer and do it for just ten minutes. You will have gotten started on your task, and may feel like sticking with it. If that is is case, stay with it. If not, you at least have a start in the right direction. Consider another ten-minute increment, or move on to another subject area and then come back.
2. **Use your phone.** If you have to remember something, like to take out the trash, do the dishes, pack your lunch, meet a teacher, or turn in your homework, record a reminder in your own voice telling you to do it. This eliminates others (parents) having to nag you. I know for a fact that a parent's nagging can have the same effect as nails down a chalkboard. (For those of you who don't know what a chalkboard is, you can look it up online.) Nails running across the surface of a chalkboard generate a screeching sound that makes you cringe. I know that parental reminders (nagging) make all teens cringe and react with defiance.
3. **Hang a whiteboard in your place of study.** Write down your to-do list and check it off upon completion of each task. This keeps you focused and holds you accountable to your list. Parents can monitor your list and keep updated on your progress without having to interrupt (nag) you.
4. **Make a playlist of your favorite study tunes.** You can find pre-made study lists online or you can compose your own. A nice gentle background beat can help you pace your brain's tempo and reduce distractions. Here are my only guidelines: nothing harsh, no heavy metal, and no lyrics. Music has an altering effect on the brain, and harsh sounds produce harsh emotions and have a harsh impact on your cells, which negatively alters your mood, emotions, and brain performance. Lyrics are nice in real life, and I really enjoy them too. However, words occupy space in your working memory and therefore reduce your brain's working memory capacity when you're performing brain-based tasks like reading or problem-solving. If you're organizing your room, that's a whole different story. Use those lyrics and put on something fun. Most of my clients have separate playlists for study, reading, and organizing tasks.

5. **Ritualize, ritualize, ritualize.** The more routinely you perform a task at set times, the greater the likelihood of it being pleasant and get accomplished. Create morning rituals--a set of three things you do each morning, and evening rituals--three things you do every night. Your ritual list might include: charge laptop, pack backpack, fill water bottles, 30 minutes of exercise, meditation, HeartMath®, review schedule, consume a hot beverage, etc. Make up your own. If starting a brand new habit, such as morning exercise, make it small to start. B.J. Fogg is a behavioral change expert who recommends that you start small, attach your new habit to one that already exists, and celebrate your small victories. Visit his website at *www.tinyhabits.com* to register your new habit and then follow his steps to make your new habit happen. Voilà! Instant accountability.

Having a coach means finding the best tips for you and empowering you to choose the tools you like and will continue to use. What I've found has worked for everyone is individually tailored plans that are fashioned collaboratively, between client and coach, over a period of time. No one system really works forever, but there is a combination of tools that works best for you, right now, that will change as you change and grow.

Once you think you have found a coach, try him or her out for a bit. The coach should be comfortable for you to work with. If anyone blames you or shames you, move along. That will never work. If anybody offers you systems that take as long as your homework actually does, then they can move along as well.

Find somebody who listens to you, who lets you talk and describe yourself and how you perceive things. Your coach should honor who you are and listen without trying to jump in and fix things for you right away.

Your coach should also empower you to take on your own organization, time management, and decision-making. Look for someone that gradually transitions you to being the one in charge. A coach should not be a lifelong commitment, but rather a guide to get you to your beautiful destination of improved performance, confidence, and radiance.

Bonus:

Test-Taking Guide

Besides compliance with deadlines and staying on top of your workload, tests play a major role in communicating what we have learned. Please think of tests as opportunities to demonstrate all that you have learned and are learning. If you keep up with your assignments, advocate for yourself, use the reading guidelines, and practice positive thinking habits, you are already in better shape. Here are the steps I recommend for better success when taking tests.

1. Create an information map on a blank sheet of paper before you even look at your test. First and foremost it's important to get your steps, your details, your formulas, and your memorized facts out on paper before your begin your test. Why? Because you will not be requiring your brain to do two tasks at the same time. Most tests ask you to solve problems using what you know. If you are simultaneously trying to retrieve data and apply it in a problem-solving situation, you are increasing the load on your brain (or, in other words, you are over-taxing your working memory capacity). By **dividing it up** into different tasks, **the retrieval part first**, all the stuff you write down, and then **the problem-solving part,** you are increasing your chances of doing both parts well.
2. Read the test all the way through first. While you might be tempted to get started right away, try this brain-hack out. Read all the questions first, all the way through. Doing so provides your brain extra time to break down, retrieve and organize information even before you attempt to answer any questions. The minute you see the question, your brain will automatically start to work, whether you want it to or not. By the time you come back around to the question to answer it, your brain has already worked through part of its response. That's the way the brain works. You might as well use it to your advantage.
3. Underline key words in the instructions and questions. So many "wrong" responses are based on misreading the question. I cannot tell you how many tests I've reviewed with students where they've provided a very correct sum when a difference was asked for, or where they've provided a very eloquent essay that did not address the question.

4. Pace yourself and breathe. After you look over the test, decide how much time to allocate to each part. Check in with yourself every few minutes to ensure that your breath is flowing. This will help oxygenate your brain and make sure that your heart and brain are cooperating for optimal efficiency.
5. Use a 3-4 item checklist to help you avoid your common errors on tests. Use the information map from Step 1 to write these down. This checklist may include: I have a topic sentence. I have written down the proper units of measure (such as lbs, or per square inch). My verbs agree with the subject. I have followed all directions. I have checked my punctuation and spelling. I have filled in the correct bubble completely. I have answered all questions (except when getting penalized for a wrong answer).
6. Plant your feet on the floor and imagine they have roots reaching deep into the Earth. This, quite literally, keeps you grounded and in the present moment, reducing your mind's tendency to wander.

Wrapping It All Up

So now it's time to wrap everything up, like a gift. It's time to start viewing your unique qualities as a learner as a gift to yourself and to this world. Your own learning style is a part of you and there is nothing wrong with you. Accept and embrace who you are as a person and as a learner. I have not given you any tools to change who you are, but rather tools to navigate yourself as a learner and to express yourself with courage and confidence.

We are all different and there is no single path that works for everybody. Take the words that you like, look for more when you need them. Speak your truth, ask for help. Most of all, be proud of who you are. I already am.

With Tremendous Love,
Dr. Donah

Some Helpful Websites to Visit:

mycogmed.com

iheart2learn.com

additudemag.com

thelifelinecenter.com

heartmath.org

choosemyplate.gov

tinyhabits.com

CPSIA information can be obtained
at www.ICGtesting.com
Printed in the USA
LVOW06s0858131117
556088LV00011B/82/P